UP

Writing a New Chapter
of Joy and Laughter

By Beth Jones

Harrison House
Tulsa, OK

Up: Writing a New Chapter of Joy and Laughter
ISBN 13: 978-160683-641-5
Copyright © 2010, 2014 by Beth Jones
www.jeffandbethjones.org

Published by Harrison House Publishers
Tulsa, OK 74145
www.harrisonhouse.com

CONTENTS

CHAPTER 1
When the Sky Is Not Blue

Got the blues? Feeling bummed out? Down in the dumps? Fighting discouragement or depression?

You're not alone.

If you've experienced a set back or disappointment lately, it can knock the wind out of your sails. If you've lost a loved one or are grieving a loss, you can feel heavy-hearted. If you've felt isolated, overlooked or rejected, then you know what an invitation to a pity party looks like.

Depression is a big problem these days, whether in the form of a mild case of the blues, clinical depression or severe depression. Many people need encouragement to find happiness and joy in their lives. It doesn't seem to matter whether you're a teen or adult, male or female, single or married, or have children or not—at times, everyone is tempted to get down.

What are some warning signs of depression? How do you know if you are facing severe depression or a mild case of being down in the dumps? If your answer to more than one of the following questions is 'yes,' this study will encourage you. You may also want to seek additional support.

Locate Yourself

Have your sleeping and eating habits changed recently?

Do you feel detached, confused or apathetic about life in general?

Does your situation feel hopeless?

Do you want to run away?

Are you unable to cope with daily life without the help of prescription drugs or intoxication?

Are you jealous or envious of friends who are reaching higher toward their dreams and desires?

Does the sky of your life always seem gray?

Perhaps you wonder if things could be different for you. Is it possible to be "up" in a down world? Will your sky ever be blue again? Does God have real answers? The good news is that God cares, and He has given us real answers through His Word to help us. In addition, He's gifted and empowered professionals to also assist us.

How I Learned This Lesson

I remember a season of the blues during my junior year in college. I was a nice, happy-go-lucky Christian college student with plans to become a dentist. I had just spent twelve weeks doing beach evangelism and discipleship training with a campus ministry on a summer project in New Hampshire. It was a life changing summer of stretching, sharing Christ and growing in my faith. I returned to college as a junior and was on fire, sold out, and ready to serve God with my life! Coming off that summer project and into the first semester of my junior year, I had a powerful encounter with the Lord. He called me to the ministry by quickening Romans 10:13-15 to my heart and giving me a "mini-vision" of what I'd be doing someday. That fall semester was a marked time in my spiritual growth and personal destiny. I was excited about God, and I wanted to spend my life doing eternal things.

Little did I know—the enemy would immediately try to quench my zeal and commitment to God. Soon my happy-go-lucky disposition was attacked and I found myself feeling depressed, bummed out and frustrated. I didn't quite know what was going on at the time; the only way I can describe it was that it seemed that negative thoughts were bombarding my mind and I felt blue for no specific reason. I eventually realized that many times the reason for an attack of discouragement or depression is because God has great plans for us and the devil perceives that God is up to something so he tries to short-circuit God's plan. This went on and off for several months. I loved the Lord with all my heart. I was reading my Bible, praying, and was committed to serving Him, yet I was living a defeated Christian life in my thoughts and emotions. I didn't know what to do. As I sought the Lord, He began to show me what I was dealing with and how to get set free from the blues. I will share some of these strategies in this Bible study.

> **NUGGET:** Some of you may be facing more severe causes and types of depression. If you've lost a loved one or have experienced divorce or a tragedy of some kind, you may be in a time of heartbreaking grief. If you're feeling overwhelmed and anxious or if you've experienced some type of traumatic stress, you may feel like a prisoner to the oppressive power of depression. Again, you might benefit from getting some professional and/or pastoral help to walk you through the process of healing and recovery.

When it comes to the normal course of our lives, the Bible tells us to "Rejoice with those who rejoice, and weep with those who weep" (Romans 12:15, NKJV). In Ecclesiastes 3:4, the Bible talks about "a time to weep and a time to laugh, a time to mourn and a time to dance" (NIV). That means there will be both rejoicing times and weeping times in our lives. That's normal. There is a time to weep or mourn and we need to comfort one another in those times in order to get back to times of joy and rejoicing. Be encouraged to know that the time to laugh and dance will come. After a loss or tragedy, people often feel guilty if they laugh or dance, so as a result they almost become locked in a prison of soberness and sadness. Remember, there is a time for weeping and mourning, and that time has a beginning and an end, because we know from God's Word that He wants most of your lifetime to be spent in fullness of joy.

Our focus in this study will be on living in the "up" side of life and choosing joy, rejoicing, laughing and dancing to help lift you out of a season of weeping, mourning, sadness, discouragement and depression. We are going to focus our attention on general principles from God's Word that will help us enjoy a life of joy and peace. Fortunately, God knows you and your circumstances intimately and He's sent the Holy Spirit to be your Helper, Counselor and Comforter. As you purpose to study and obey God's Word on this subject, expect the Holy Spirit to lead and guide you into a customized plan for freedom from depression and expect to be embraced by the One who loves you most!

Depression and Discouragement Is Epidemic

Commercials and advertisements aimed at adults and children for mood-enhancing drugs bombard us on television and in print. The National Institute of Mental Health (NIMH) stated, "Research has shown that in the United States about nineteen million people—one in ten adults—experience depression each year, and nearly two-thirds do not get the help they need."[1]

When I conducted an Internet search on "depression," fifteen million resources were at my fingertips in five seconds. Most sources said that depression is twice as common in women as in men. Everyone deals with a certain degree of feeling blue due to normal life experiences. The loss of a loved one, continual stress caused by financial pressures, a business or marriage failure, uncertain economy, and health or family problems can cause differing degrees of sadness. When these blue feelings begin to interrupt your normal ability to function for an extended time period and in a greater intensity, it's time to recognize the potential for a more serious problem that must be treated in some way.

Most experts agree on the basic symptoms of depression which include:

- Persistent sad, anxious or "empty" mood.
- Loss of energy, interest or pleasure in activities, including sex.
- Diminished ability to enjoy oneself.
- Restlessness, irritability or excessive crying.

- Feelings of guilt, worthlessness, helplessness, hopelessness and pessimism.

- Sleeping too much or too little, early-morning awakening.

- Appetite and/or weight loss or overeating and weight gain.

- Decreased energy, fatigue, feeling "slowed down."

- Thoughts of death or suicide, or suicide attempts.

- Difficulty concentrating, remembering or making decisions.

- Slowed or fuzzy thinking.

- Persistent physical symptoms that do not respond to treatment, such as headaches, digestive disorders and chronic pain.

Just what is depression? The NIMH says, "Life is full of emotional ups and downs. But when the 'down times' are long lasting or interfere with your ability to function, you may be suffering from a common, serious illness—depression. Clinical depression affects mood, mind, body, and behavior."[2]

Depression can be caused by many things—genetic factors, biochemical factors, environmental factors, life stress factors, personality and social factors, life season factors, relationship and work factors, premenstrual, postpartum and menopausal factors, cultural factors, abuse and victimization factors, poverty, sickness and disease, or a blatant spiritual attack from the devil.

Thank God for the insight He has given to medical and mental health professionals. They are doing their best to provide treatment for those affected by the blues. The most commonly used treatments for depression are antidepressant medication, psychotherapy, or a combination of the two. Sometimes these treatments are quite effective in helping people temporarily. While these treatments are important, God offers us His supernatural help with the promise that His joy and peace can replace depression and discouragement.

Let's turn our attention to God's Word to discover His plan for lifting us up. As you read His words, let your heart and mind embrace them. Then as you meditate on them, they will get down in your spirit!

A Spirit of Heaviness

1. Isaiah 61:1-3

    In this passage, underline the words that describe depression and the blues.

    > The Spirit of the Lord GOD is upon Me, because the LORD has anointed Me to preach good tidings to the poor; He has sent me to heal the brokenhearted, to proclaim liberty to the captives, and the opening of the prison to those who are bound; to proclaim the acceptable year of the LORD, and the day of vengeance of our God; to comfort all who mourn, to console those who mourn in Zion, to give them beauty for ashes, the oil of joy for mourning, the garment of praise for the spirit of heaviness; that they may be called trees of righteousness, the planting of the LORD, that He may be glorified. (NKJV)

    Another way to describe depression, the blues or being bummed out is with the phrase "a spirit of heaviness." Sometimes a person just feels heavy—emotionally, mentally, physically and even spiritually. God wants us to be free from a spirit of heaviness.

    What does God tell the poor?

    What does He do for the broken-hearted?

    What does God want for those held captive?

What does He want for those in prison?

What does He do for those who mourn?

What does He give in place of ashes?

What does He give in place of the spirit of heaviness?

God understands the reality of the blues, depression and a heavy heart. He realizes that these things make us poor, brokenhearted, captives, prisoners, mournful, covered with ashes and heavy-hearted. Thankfully, He provides freedom from all of these things.

Can you relate to any of these things? If so, describe which ones:

2. Acts 10:38

   Underline the phrase "oppressed of the devil."

   How God anointed Jesus of Nazareth with the Holy Ghost and with power: who went about doing good, and healing all that were oppressed of the devil; for God was with him. (KJV)

What did God anoint Jesus with?

What did Jesus do?

Did He leave anyone out?

What do you think it means to be oppressed of the devil?

In what ways is depression oppressive?

Do you believe Jesus is still going about doing good and healing all who are oppressed by the devil?

The good news is that although Jesus is not on the earth today physically, He is still alive and healing and freeing people from all oppression, including depression.

3. Hebrews 13:8

Underline the words "yesterday," "today" and "forever."

Jesus Christ the same yesterday, and to day, and for ever. (KJV)

Has Jesus changed?

If He did something good yesterday, will He do it today?

How long is Jesus the same?

NUGGET: Jesus is the same! If Jesus went about doing good and healing all who were oppressed yesterday, that means that Jesus is still freeing people from oppression today. Jesus sets people free through His Word and by His Spirit. Sometimes this comes instantly and people are supernaturally delivered from depression. Other times, He sets people free by giving them Holy Spirit inspired ideas, knowledge or wisdom that leads them to do any number of things—change their eating habits or their environment, seek professional Christian counseling or medical help, set personal boundaries, or better manage their interpersonal relationships. Jesus shows us from His Word how to think and how to speak in such a way as to not only be free from the oppression of de-pression and disappointment, but to stay free and walk in joy and gladness!

If a sense of discouragement, the blues, being bummed out, depression, dis-appointment or a heavy heart has plagued you—you are not alone. God has the help you need!

Godly People Feel Depressed at Times

Sometimes it's encouraging to know that the challenges you are facing have also been experienced by other people who loved God. David expressed his heart before God throughout the psalms, and he let us know that a sense of depression often assaulted him. His response was to pray and seek God for help. Listen to his cry in Psalm 143:7-8: *"Come quickly, LORD, and answer me, for my depression deepens. Don't turn away from me, or I will die. Let me hear of your unfailing love each morning, for I am trusting you. Show me where to walk, for I give myself to you" (NLT).*

1. Psalm 42:3-11

    Underline the phrases "in the dumps," "crying the blues," "I'll be praising again" and "He puts a smile on my face."

    I'm on a diet of tears — tears for breakfast, tears for supper. All day long people knock at my door, pestering, "Where is this God of yours?"

    These are the things I go over and over, emptying out the pockets of my life. I was always at the head of the worshiping crowd, right out in front, Leading them all, eager to arrive and worship, shouting praises, singing thanksgiving—celebrating, all of us, God's feast! Why are you down in the dumps, dear soul?

    Why are you crying the blues? Fix my eyes on God—soon I'll be praising again. He puts a smile on my face. He's my God.

    When my soul is in the dumps, I rehearse everything I know of you, from Jordan depths to Hermon heights, including Mount Mizar. Chaos calls to chaos, to the tune of whitewater rapids. Your breaking surf, your thundering breakers crash and crush me. Then God promises to love me all day, sing songs all through the night! My life is God's prayer.

Sometimes I ask God, my rock-solid God, "Why did you let me down? Why am I walking around in tears, harassed by enemies?" They're out for the kill, these tormentors with their obscenities, taunting day after day, "Where is this God of yours?"

Why are you down in the dumps, dear soul? Why are you crying the blues? Fix my eyes on God—soon I'll be praising again. He puts a smile on my face. He's my God. (The Message)

This entire psalm is about the discouragement the psalmist was experiencing.

What symptoms of depression do you see in this psalm?

What was the solution in verses 4-8, 11?

Have you ever had a conversation like this with God? I love David's honesty—while he freely shared his heart and discouragement with the Lord, he always reminded himself of what he knew to be true about God and His goodness to him.

2. Psalm 43:5

Underline the words "discouraged" and "sad."

Why am I discouraged? Why is my heart so sad? I will put my hope in God! I will praise him again—my Savior and my God! (NLT)

What did David ask?

To feel discouraged, depressed or down is not necessarily a sin, but to stay in the "mulligrubs" is not God's plan. He is our help and way out.

NUGGET: It's helpful when we're discouraged to discover and isolate the reason we feel this way. The enemy doesn't know everything, but he does seem to know where we are weak. He recognizes our weak links and looks for a way to push our buttons and trigger our weaknesses to bring on discouragement. It's our job to strengthen those weak areas. For example, if the enemy knows that having patience is a weakness in our lives, he will find ways to test our patience with the hope that we'll fall into depression and discouragement.

Have you noticed any areas of weakness in your own life? If so, describe the way the enemy tries to capitalize on those areas.

Can you isolate any particular reasons that you feel blue?

What two things did David say, "I will do"?

NUGGET: Hope and praise are two of your best weapons against the blues. When your hope is deferred, it makes you heartsick. God wants you to hope. But you have to do it by faith. Hoping in God and His Word gives you the blueprint for a better future. To stir up your hope, remind yourself of what can be. Rehearse your dreams. Then praise God, because praising God is your next step of faith. Praise Him for what you know to be true, even when your feelings and circumstances are contrary. Praise the Lord for Who He is. Praise the Lord for all that He has done. By faith, praise the Lord for all that He will do, and you will sense His Presence filling your life.

3. 1 Kings 19:1-21

In this lengthy passage, underline all the things God said to Elijah when he became very depressed as he faced persecution from his enemies, Ahab and Jezebel.

> *And Ahab told Jezebel all that Elijah had done, also how he had executed all the prophets with the sword. Then Jezebel sent a messenger to Elijah, saying, "So let the gods do to me, and more also, if I do not make your life as the life of one of them by tomorrow about this time." And when he saw that, he arose and ran for his life, and went to Beersheba, which belongs to Judah, and left his servant there.*

> *But he himself went a day's journey into the wilderness, and came and sat down under a broom tree. And he prayed that he might die, and said, "It is enough! Now, LORD, take my life, for I am no better than my fathers!"*

> *Then as he lay and slept under a broom tree, suddenly an angel touched him, and said to him, "Arise and eat." Then he looked, and there by his head was a cake baked on coals, and a jar of water. So he ate and drank, and lay down again. And the angel of the LORD came back the second time, and touched him, and said, "Arise and eat, because the journey is too great for you." So he arose, and ate and drank; and he went in the strength of that food forty days and forty nights as far as Horeb, the mountain of God.*

> *And there he went into a cave, and spent the night in that place; and behold, the word of the LORD came to him, and He said to him, "What are you doing here, Elijah?"*

> *So he said, "I have been very zealous for the LORD God of hosts; for the children of Israel have forsaken Your covenant, torn down Your altars, and killed Your prophets with the sword. I alone am left; and they seek to take my life."*

Then He said, "Go out, and stand on the mountain before the LORD." And behold, the LORD passed by, and a great and strong wind tore into the mountains and broke the rocks in pieces before the LORD, but the LORD was not in the wind; and after the wind an earthquake, but the LORD was not in the earthquake; and after the earthquake a fire, but the LORD was not in the fire; and after the fire a still small voice.

So it was, when Elijah heard it, that he wrapped his face in his mantle and went out and stood in the entrance of the cave. Suddenly a voice came to him, and said, "What are you doing Here, Elijah?"

And he said, "I have been very zealous for the LORD God of hosts; because the children of Israel have forsaken Your covenant, torn down Your altars, and killed Your prophets with the sword. I alone am left; and they seek to take my life."

Then the LORD said to him: "Go, return on your way to the Wilderness of Damascus; and when you arrive, anoint Hazael as king over Syria. Also you shall anoint Jehu the son of Nimshi as king over Israel. And Elisha the son of Shaphat of Abel Meholah you shall anoint as prophet in your place. It shall be that whoever escapes the sword of Hazael, Jehu will kill; and whoever escapes the sword of Jehu, Elisha will kill. Yet I have reserved seven thousand in Israel, all whose knees have not bowed to Baal, and every mouth that has not kissed him."

So he departed from there, and found Elisha the son of Shaphat, who was plowing with twelve yoke of oxen before him, and he was with the twelfth. Then Elijah passed by him and threw his mantle on him. And he left the oxen and ran after Elijah, and said, "Please let me kiss my father and my mother, and then I will follow you."

And he said to him, "Go back again, for what have I done to you?"

So Elisha turned back from him, and took a yoke of oxen and slaughtered them and boiled their flesh, using the oxen's equipment, and gave it to the people, and they ate. Then he arose and followed Elijah, and became his servant. (NKJV)

What did Elijah experience in verse 1?

The prophet Elijah was tempted to be discouraged and depressed after a great victory. God's power had just been manifested and had blown away the Baal worshippers. You would think that Elijah would be flying high after this great ministerial success. Everyone, except one woman, thought Elijah was God's man. Jezebel hated Elijah and wanted him dead.

NUGGET: It's interesting that often after a great success or a great time of consecration in life and ministry, we are most vulnerable to depression or discouragement. Hundreds of people can say, "Praise the Lord, you did a great job." And yet, one "Jezebel-type" can be in the crowd and write you a nasty note, send you a critical e-mail or just get in your face and question your motives and purpose, and nullify all the good. Perhaps you just recommitted yourself to God and His plan and you've reached a new place of consecration, when suddenly you find yourself feeling the enemy's attacks on your confidence and abilities in an effort to get you down.

In verse 2, what did Jezebel want to do to Elijah?

In verses 3-5, what was Elijah's response?

In verses 5-8, how did God encourage Elijah?

Perhaps some of the first steps we need to take at times are simply improving our diet and resting. God used an angel to help Elijah eat and rest so he could be strengthened.

What role does diet or sleeping habits play in your sense of well-being?

In verses 9-10, Elijah was discouraged again. What did he do and say?

In verses 11-12, what did the Lord reveal to Elijah?

The most important thing in life is hearing from God and following Him. When you're discouraged, it's a good idea to spend extra time with God in the Bible and allow His Word to saturate and marinate your mind. As you read the Scriptures, expect Him to speak a word in due season to your heart.

In verses 13-14, Elijah tried to invite God to his pity party.

Describe this pity party in your own words:

In verses 15-18, how did God respond to Elijah's pity party?

God barely acknowledged Elijah's whine! It's almost as if God disregarded it and just distracted him from his problem. God let Elijah know that the premise that had him depressed was wrong, so he straightened out his thinking.

NUGGET: Notice that God put Elijah to work! I believe the Lord knew when Elijah operated in the calling that God had for his life that he would be refreshed, so He immediately sent Elijah back to work. There is something really healthy and energizing about operating in the gifts and callings God has in our lives. When we are not utilizing our God-given gifts, there is a feeling of dissatisfaction and unfulfillment. Often, we find ourselves depressed because we are not walking in the destiny, purpose and fullness of God's will for our lives.

We once talked to a gal who was gifted in organizational things. One day, as she was organizing an event, she made the comment that "it just made her hormones happy to organize things." She was operating in her gift and it made her happy. When we operate outside of our gifts for an extended period of time, we will feel empty and ineffective. I believe there are multitudes of Christians who love God with all of their hearts, but they are not fulfilling God's plan for their lives. They have their own agendas and plans. Some of these people are very successful in business, the arts, medicine and homemaking, yet they struggle with depression and a sense of missing their purpose.

God knew that Elijah would find encouragement in fulfilling his destiny. I don't believe the Lord was being cold-hearted, instead He was trying to get some gladness flowing into Elijah's life!

In verses 19-21, what did Elijah do?

It's interesting that the end of this story has Elisha ministering to Elijah. God was going to allow Elijah to leave a legacy, and Elisha was the one God was using to bring that about. There is no better way to get out of depression than to get the focus off of ourselves and onto others. Mentoring others and leaving a legacy is a great way to get our eyes off our personal issues and onto the needs of others.

Who's in your life that you can and should reach out to?

Who are you mentoring?

What type of legacy do you plan to leave?

Scriptures to Meditate On

How sweet are Your words to my taste,
Sweeter than honey to my mouth!

Psalm 119:103, NKJV

Yet in all these things we are more than conquerors
through Him who loved us.

Romans 8:37, NKJV

Group Discussion

1. Describe a time in your life when you were blue, bummed or depressed. What factors contributed to that season? How did you communicate with the Lord?

2. Describe the current culture and reliance on alcohol and mood-enhancing drugs. Do you think there is an overemphasis on drugs? Do you believe drugs help people? What is your view on this?

3. Describe the role of your diet, rest, work, stress, boundaries, and your personal walk with the Lord and fulfilling your calling, in terms of causing or curing symptoms of depression. Has the Lord led you to made adjustments in any of these areas?

---

[1] *Psychiatric Disorders in America, The Epidemiologic Catchment Area Study,* Robins LN and Regier DA (Eds), (New York: The Free Press, 1990).

[2] Ibid

CHAPTER 2
The Problem With Pity Parties

It would be nice if God would wave His "Tinker Bell wand" and sprinkle us with happy dust, wouldn't it?

It would be great if we could click our heels like Dorothy and wake up feeling joyful, right?

It would be encouraging if a few friends would join us when we throw a pity party, wouldn't it?

The truth is that if we are going to be happy and joyful, we are going to have to start by encouraging ourselves in the Lord. To overcome feelings of depression and discouragement, we have to accept the fact that we are responsible for our happiness. It's not up to God, our mom, dad, husband, wife, children, best friend, president, journalist or pastor. It's up to us! We must take responsibility for seeking the Lord and choosing His will.

When we look to everyone else to make us happy, we will be disappointed. In fact, we may need to lower the bar of expectation we have for others to make us happy. As wonderful as our family and friends are to us, they cannot make us happy. It's not their job. Of course, God uses people to encourage us, but ultimately He wants us to be independently dependent upon Him—and Him alone.

If you've been continually disappointed with people, it's time to do a 180-degree turn and change your thinking and expectations. You can count on it— people will disappoint you! God will make sure of it, because He is a jealous God and He alone is to be the joy and rejoicing of our hearts. When our expectation is from the Lord and when we learn to encourage ourselves in Him, He will lead us to a place of great contentment and happiness. When we are in that place of contentment, He will often add God-breathed friendships into our lives.

Let's look at this subject of encouraging yourself.

Encourage Yourself

1. 1 Samuel 30:1-8

    Underline the phrase "David encouraged himself in the Lord."

    > *And it came to pass, when David and his men were come to Ziklag on the third day, that the Amalekites had invaded the south, and Ziklag, and smitten Ziklag, and burned it with fire; and had taken the women captives, that were therein: they slew not any, either great or small, but carried them away, and went on their way.*

    > *So David and his men came to the city, and, behold, it was burned with fire; and their wives, and their sons, and their daughters, were taken captives. Then David and the people that were with him lifted up their voice and wept, until they had no more power to weep.*

    > *And David's two wives were taken captives, Ahinoam the Jezreelitess, and Abigail the wife of Nabal the Carmelite. And David was greatly distressed; for the people spake of stoning him, because the soul of all the people was grieved, every man for his sons and for his daughters: but David encouraged himself in the LORD his God.*

    > *And David said to Abiathar the priest, Ahimelech's son, I pray thee, bring me hither the ephod. And Abiathar brought thither the ephod to David. And David inquired at the LORD, saying,*

Shall I pursue after this troop? shall I overtake them? And he answered him, Pursue: for thou shalt surely overtake them, and without fail recover all. (KJV)

David had left Ziklag and led his men to fight the Philistines. When they returned to Ziklag, they found the Amalekites had devastated their homes and families.

What happened to David and his people?

Can you imagine the heartbreak and anger? Their homes and city had been burned down, and their wives and children were gone—abducted and kidnapped. It was heartbreaking. Put yourself in their shoes. A great sense of despair and depression must have flooded their hearts.

What was their response to this tragedy?

In the end of this passage, things went from bad to worse. Not only was David in turmoil personally, but he also became the scapegoat for everyone else's pain.

In verse 6, what were the people talking about doing?

What was David's response in light of this new threat?

Encouraged: this means to strengthen, to prevail, to harden, to be strong, to become strong, to be courageous, to be firm, grow firm, to be resolute, to be sure.[1]

There are times when we just have to encourage ourselves in the Lord. No one else can or will do this for us. We have to strengthen ourselves in God. We have to toughen up. Get some grit. Harden ourselves to despair and depression. We must make ourselves be resolute and courageous. It's not always easy, yet it is required.

What do you think David did to encourage himself?

How do you encourage yourself in the Lord?

In verse 8, what did David do?

Prayer is huge! When we seek the Lord and inquire of Him in the midst of tough times, He directs and lifts us up.

No Complaining

1. Philippians 2:14-15

    Underline the things we are to avoid.

    Do everything without complaining or arguing, so that you may become blameless and pure, children of God without fault in a crooked and depraved generation, in which you shine like stars in the universe. (NIV)

THE PROBLEM WITH PITY PARTIES

When do we get to grumble, complain or murmur?

What does it prove when we choose to avoid the negative, pessimistic ways of thinking and talking?

You might be thinking, *Yeah, but what about (insert your specifics here)? Yeah, but you don't know my life or my boss or my spouse or my kids or my situation! I have a right to complain and murmur. Anyone in my shoes would do the same thing. It's just not possible to be happy and joyful in my situation. I have a right to feel like this!* Anytime we defend our right to complain, to be a victim, to be negative, or to remain discouraged or depressed—we are establishing a stronghold. It's an unhealthy way to view and live life. If we make a quality decision to rid ourselves of this right, depression won't be able to have a stronghold on us. That's encouraging!

2. Luke 7:31-33

   Underline the words "complain," "happy" and "sad."

   > "To what can I compare the people of this generation?" Jesus asked. "How can I describe them? They are like children playing a game in the public square. They complain to their friends, 'We played wedding songs, and you didn't dance, so we played funeral songs, but you didn't weep.' (NLT)

   What did these children do?

Take Responsibility

1. James 5:13

    Underline the words that tell us the responsibility of the believer.

    Is any among you afflicted? let him pray. (KJV)

    What are you supposed to do if you are afflicted?

    Are you supposed to call the prayer chain and ask everyone else to pray for you? Are you supposed to lie down and have a pity party? No, the first thing we are to do when we are afflicted is pray! It's our responsibility to pray about our own issues. Sure, after we have prayed, it's great to get others to agree with us, but *we* are to pray if we are afflicted. It's our responsibility to pray for ourselves.

2. Isaiah 40:29-31

    Underline the words "weak," "no might," "faint," "weary" and "fall."

    He gives power to the weak, and to those who have no might He increases strength. Even the youths shall faint and be weary, and the young men shall utterly fall, But those who wait on the LORD shall renew their strength; they shall mount up with wings like eagles, they shall run and not be weary, they shall walk and not faint. (NKJV)

    God gives power and strength to whom?

If we want our strength renewed and our spirits lifted up, what do we need to do?

When we wait on the Lord, what is the result?

How do you wait on the Lord?

3. Isaiah 52:2

    Underline the phrase "shake yourself."

    > Shake yourself from the dust; arise, sit [erect in a dignified place], O Jerusalem; loose yourself from the bonds of your neck, O captive Daughter of Zion. (AMP)

    After being in bondage for years, what did God tell the captives to do?

    Sometimes we need to grab ourselves by the back of the neck and shake off the oppression that the enemy tries to bring upon us. When you are tempted to feel sorry for yourself, stop and shake yourself! Don't allow discouragement and depression to keep you in captivity.

4. Galatians 6:9

    Underline the phrase "don't get discouraged."

*And let us not get tired of doing what is right, for after a while
we will reap a harvest of blessing if we don't get discouraged
and give up. (TLB)*

When you are encouraging yourself, don't get discouraged! You might
not notice any difference in your life the first time you start to encourage
yourself. If you've been down in the dumps for three weeks, it's going to
take more than five minutes to move into a perpetual state of joy. Stay
with it and your soul will turn!

What does this verse tell us NOT to do?

What is promised?

What is our responsibility?

Are you ready to sow happiness and joy seeds into your own life?

5. Jeremiah 30:19

Underline the phrase "depression days are over."

*Thanksgivings will pour out of the windows; laughter will spill
through the doors. Things will get better and better. Depression days are over. They'll thrive, they'll flourish. The days of
contempt will be over. (The Message)*

THE PROBLEM WITH PITY PARTIES

What happened to these people when God brought them out of captivity?

Scriptures to Meditate On

Finally, my brethren, be strong in the Lord and in the power of His might.
Ephesians 6:10, NKJV

Do everything without complaining or arguing,
so that you may become blameless and pure,
children of God without fault in a crooked and depraved generation,
in which you shine like stars in the universe.

Philippians 2:14-15, NIV

Group Discussion

1. Describe a time in your life when you looked to others for your happiness. Were you disappointed? What did you learn?

2. Describe the way you encourage yourself in the Lord. What do you do to seek the Lord and find encouragement?

3. Describe the importance of taking responsibility for the happiness you experience in life. Have you observed in your life, or the lives of others, the results of not taking this responsibility?

[1] Joseph H. Thayer, *Thayer's Greek-English Lexicon* (New York: Baker Academic, 1977). www.biblestudytools.com/search/?q=encouraged&s = references&rc=LEX&rc2=LEX+GRK. Francis Brown, SR Driver and Charles Briggs, Brown-Driver-Briggs Hebrew and English Lexicon, (New York: Snowball Publishing, 2011), www.biblestudytools.com/search/?q= encouraged&s= references&rc=LEX&rc2=LEX+HEB.

CHAPTER 3
The Things You Could Think if Only You Tried

Forrest Gump understood something about the importance of what he thought and what he said, when he said, "That's all I have to say about that." This should be our motto, too! Both what we think and what we say are huge in determining whether we will have a life of joy or a life down in the dumps.

While the medical and mental health professions are doing their best to provide treatment for those affected by the blues and depression through antidepressant medication, psychotherapy, or a combination of the two, the question remains, "Does God offer us His supernatural help for overcoming depression and discouragement with the promise of authentic results? Are drugs and psychotherapy the only options? Does the Bible reveal God's strategy for being set free from depression?" The answer is yes! Depression, discouragement and disappointment are not God's highest and best. His best for us is a life of joy!

Before we study the importance of our thought life, why not take a moment and imagine your life with a pep in your step and joy in your heart!

> NUGGET: Is it possible that God, through His Word, could do a work in your spirit, mind, emotions, and even in chemical pathways of the human brain, that would affect your behavior and disposition? Absolutely! With God, all things are possible! As you cooperate with Him, His Word effectually works within you. Let's look at two important areas: What are you thinking? What are you saying?

Your thoughts and words will dictate your level of depression or joy.

What Do You Think?

The Bible is full of exhortations on what we think. Our thoughts determine our beliefs, and our beliefs determine our attitudes and actions. It's a domino effect—and it all begins with what we think.

1. Philippians 4:8

    Underline the words that describe the things we are to think on.

    > *Finally, brethren, whatsoever things are true, whatsoever things are honest, whatsoever things are just, whatsoever things are pure, whatsoever things are lovely, whatsoever things are of good report; if there be any virtue, and if there be any praise, think on these things. (KJV)*

    What eight things are we supposed to think and meditate on?

    Is there any room in this verse for dwelling on depressing, sad, or blue thoughts?

    Is there any place in this verse for being negative or for having a pity party in your thoughts?

    > *Someone might say, "Well, it's true. I am depressed and my life is a mess . . . and the Bible says to think on things that are true . . . so it's true, I'm depressed!" Here's a question to consider: Which is truer, your thoughts and experiences*

or God's Word? Think on the higher truth of God's Word and allow your mind to be renewed.

NUGGET: Let's talk about truth versus facts. This is so important. If we want to walk in the freedom God provides, we have to live by the truth. Often, the facts are contradictory to the truth found in God's Word. It may be a fact that we are bummed out and life feels rotten at the moment, but the truth of God's Word according to Psalm 118:24 is, ***This is the day the Lord has made and I will rejoice and be glad in it.*** So, although it's a fact that we are bummed and discouraged, the truth is that this is the day the Lord has made and we choose to rejoice and be glad anyway. Can you see the importance of choosing God's truth over symptomatic and circumstantial facts?

This separates those who walk in victory from those who live in defeat. At times, people feel they are being dishonest or lying when they choose the truth over the facts. Don't let the voice of the accuser trip you up. Choose the truth of God's Word in every situation—at all times. Facts are subject to change, truth is not. When the facts are not congruent with the truth, we have to make a decision. Which one will we think on? Which one will we choose to act on? It's always wise to choose truth. Jesus said the truth will set you free. The facts will keep you in bondage. You may need to recognize the facts, but believe and act on the truth.

2. 2 Corinthians 10:3-5

In this passage, underline the things that come against our mind.

> *For though we walk in the flesh, we do not war according to the flesh. For the weapons of our warfare are not carnal but mighty in God for pulling down strongholds, casting down arguments and every high thing that exalts itself against the knowledge of God, bringing every thought into captivity to the obedience of Christ. (NKJV)*

When we are fighting a battle in our mind and emotions, we need weapons.

What kind of power do God's weapons have?

What three things do our weapons do?

_____ strongholds.

_____ arguments and every high thing.

_____ every thought.

What are we to do with our thoughts?

If you read this passage from the bottom up, notice that everything be-gins with a thought and then moves into an argument or a high thing that is set against the knowledge of God. And finally, that thought moves into a stronghold. For example, depression is a stronghold, but it doesn't start as a stronghold. It starts with a thought. If we have the thought, *I'm so bummed,* and we don't take this thought captive and make it obey the Word, this thought turns into an argument or imagination that goes against what God says. At this stage, we begin to argue for and imagine all the supporting reasons we are bummed out. We think, *After all, I have a right to be depressed. Look at my life! Here's the list of all the reasons I should be discouraged. I imagine that I'll always be depressed. God hasn't been fair to me. Where is He when I need Him? I imagine I'll be like this forever and I'll probably never be happy again.* This argument or imagination then moves into a stronghold and we begin to get into the pattern of thinking, *My life is such a mess. Nothing good happens for me. Who wouldn't be depressed?* If we don't arrest those arguments and imaginations, then—voila!—we will have established a stronghold and unless we do something about, it we'll become a negative, pessimistic and depressed person.

Can you see this progression? Thoughts move to arguments and imaginations, and eventually turn into strongholds. The good news is that this sequence will work to establish a stronghold of joy in our lives in the same way. For example, if we take a thought of joy and let it become an argument or imagination that agrees with God's Word, we can argue for this truth and imagine ourselves full of joy. Then as we continue to do this, in time, joy will become a stronghold in our lives!

3. Isaiah 26:3

   Underline the secret to enjoying God's perfect peace.

   > *You will keep him in perfect peace, whose mind is stayed on You, because he trusts in You. (NKJV)*

   If we want perfect peace in our lives, what must we do with our minds and thoughts?

   How do you keep your mind stayed on Him?

4. Acts 26:2

   Underline the phrase "I think myself happy."

   > *I think myself happy, King Agrippa, because today I shall answer for myself before you concerning all the things of which I am accused by the Jews. (NKJV)*

The Apostle Paul was a prisoner and falsely accused—he had a reason to be blue. And yet, what did he tell King Agrippa?

He could have said, "This is so unfair. I am mad and this makes me sad. Why should I be a prisoner? I have nothing to say to you, King Agrippa." But Paul chose to be happy, because he understood what a privilege it was to be a witness for Jesus Christ!

What Do You Say?

What you say is what you get! Talk therapy is God's idea. He's given us one of the most incredible tools for joy, gladness and happiness—and it's found just an inch or so below our noses! Our mouths carry power, and it's vital that our words are congruent with our thoughts and in line with God's Word. Sometimes we feel like talking in a positive and uplifting way in agreement with God's Word, and sometimes we don't. If we want our Christian life to move off the emotional roller coaster, we need to say what God says—on purpose! Let's look at this.

1. Isaiah 61:3

    Underline the antidote for the spirit of heaviness.

    To console those who mourn in Zion, to give them beauty for ashes, the oil of joy for mourning, the garment of praise for the spirit of heaviness; that they may be called trees of righteousness, the planting of the LORD, that He may be glorified. (NKJV)

    What should we do if we want to replace "ashes," "mourning" and the "spirit of heaviness"?

Praise is powerful! When was the last time you just lifted your voice at home, in your car, at church or anywhere to praise God in the midst of your discouragement? Praise God for Who He is and for what He's done for you. Do it today! Here's an assignment for you. Write down twenty things you can praise God for:

2. Psalm 100:1-2

    Underline the words "joyful shout," "gladness" and "singing."

    > *Make a joyful shout to the LORD, all you lands! Serve the LORD with gladness; come before His presence with singing. (NKJV)*

    How should we shout to the Lord?

    When was the last time you shouted to the Lord with a voice of triumph? Why not do it right now!

    How should we serve the Lord?

    How should we come before His presence?

    Be honest. How many of us have served the Lord with madness? Sadness? We sometimes serve out of guilt, duty, obligation or martyrdom, but the Lord's plan is that we serve Him with gladness!

    NUGGET: It's pretty plain, right? Gladness comes with the territory. Anytime you find yourself mad, unglad, sad or bad when serving the Lord, something's not right. So, anytime you notice gladness lacking for an extended period of time, it's time to check your heart and find out what's up.

How do you serve the Lord with gladness when your feelings are contrary?

Here are some additional suggestions for serving the Lord with joy.

First, you just choose it. You just choose to put on a happy face and say, "This is the day the Lord has made and I WILL rejoice and be glad in it!"

Second, you ponder your privilege. There is a great heart fulfillment that comes from knowing that your service to and for God is producing an eternal weight of glory! Ponder the thought . . . you GET to serve God with your life! You don't HAVE to, you GET to! How privileged we are to have been chosen by Him to bear fruit, much fruit—fruit that remains. That's enough to make us happy for the next few decades!

Third, think about the future. When this whole deal wraps up and you are face to face with the Lord Jesus—the Head of the Church—and He checks out your planner to see how you spent your life, you are going to be happy that you served Him with gladness!

3. Psalm 118:24

Underline the positive way we are to respond to each day.

> *This is the day which the LORD hath made; we will rejoice and be glad in it. (KJV)*

Who gave us this day?

What are we to do today?

4. Philippians 4:4

Underline our responsibility to be happy.

> *Rejoice in the Lord always. I will say it again: Rejoice! (NIV)*

What are we supposed to do always?

Again?

How do you rejoice?

NUGGET: This is so simple, yet so huge! The last thing we feel like doing when we are down is rejoicing, right? I remember being in a job I didn't like and having a particularly bummer day. As I sat at my desk moping and complaining, I felt that the Lord spoke to my heart and said, ***"Rejoice always."*** I didn't feel like rejoicing. Again, the thought came to me, ***"Rejoice always."*** I really didn't feel like rejoicing, but I decided to do it anyway. So, in my sad, pitiful state,

I slouched at my desk and said, *"I'm joyful."* You couldn't tell it by my face or tone of voice, that's for sure! I said it again: *"I'm joyful."* This time, I had a little more pep in my voice. I continued to say, *"I'm joyful,"* several more times and by the fifth or sixth time, I started to laugh. That simple declaration of *"I'm joyful"* on a day when I was feeling bummed out, lifted me right out of being down in the dumps.

5. Proverbs 18:21

Underline the two words that describe the power of our words.

> *The tongue has the power of life and death, and those who love it will eat its fruit. (NIV)*

What part of you has the power of life and death?

What is your mouth producing for you?

What type of fruit are you eating in life?

Do you recognize this is the fruit of what you've been saying?

Have you been saying, "I'm stressed, I'm worn out, I'm bummed," or have you heard yourself saying, "These kids are driving me crazy! My boss is ruining my life. I can't stand that waitress?"

If you've been guilty of talking like this, is it any wonder why you are feeling depressed and bummed out? What's the solution? Change the way you speak! You can't go north (joyful) and south (depressed) at the same time, so make your decision and set your tongue like a rudder and head north!

NUGGET: I have noticed something in my own life and in observing others. Just because we know some principles and truths from God's Word, doesn't mean that we are experiencing the resulting good fruit in our lives. Many people know they ought to guard their words and only speak words that edify and build up their own lives and the lives of those around them. Lots of people know they should not speak words that are counterproductive or contrary to God's Word. But the real proof of whether we know God's Word in truth, is how much of it we are putting into practice. It's not enough to just *know* what the Word says. If you want to experience a life free from depression and discouragement and full of joy and gladness, you will have to *do* the Word. Don't be like the people who hear a truth from God's Word and say, "Oh I already knew that." Be the kind of person who honestly asks himself, "Am I doing it?" According to God's Word, it's the "doers" of the Word who are blessed.

What phrases can you begin to say to turn your life in the right direction?

Scriptures to Meditate On

Death and life are in the power of the tongue,
And those who love it will eat its fruit.

Proverbs 18:21, NKJV

Do not let any unwholesome talk come out of your mouths,
but only what is helpful for building others up according to their needs,
that it may benefit those who listen.

Ephesians 4:29, NIV

Group Discussion

1. Describe how negative "facts" have robbed you or others from experiencing the "truth" of God's Word. Talk about the battle that is involved in choosing to think on the "truth," as more true than the "facts" of discouragement or depression you may face.

2. Describe the process of something going from a "thought" to an "argument or high thing that exalts itself against the knowledge of God" to a "stronghold." Discuss this process in producing negative results and in producing positive results.

3. Describe your life—the who, the what, the when, the where, the why and the how of your lifestyle—as full of joy, in fifty words.

CHAPTER 4
Going To Your Happy Place

It was a very stressful time in our lives. We were raising four young children, building a new church building and keeping up with the demands of a growing congregation. One day, I noticed that I had not laughed in a long time. I consider myself a person who laughs easily and who usually finds the humor in just about anything, but for this season, it was all work and no play—all serious and no laughter. I realized that I had gotten in a bad habit of not laughing.

To remedy the stress and seriousness that had overtaken my life, I decided to start looking for the light side. I knew I needed to get a new vision, so I searched through old boxes of photos looking for a snapshot of me laughing. When I found one, I posted that photo on our refrigerator so I could get a new image of the person I wanted to be again. It worked! Within a few weeks, I found myself laughing and enjoying this season of my life in a fresh, new way. It was confirmed when a co-worker, who heard me laugh one day said, "I love hearing you laugh; you have not laughed in a long time."

How about you? Have you laughed lately? We've all had those days, weeks, or perhaps long seasons where we just wanted to tune out all of the negativity around us and run to our happy place. Well, here's good news—Jesus wants us to live in the happy place! Have you noticed that when you are full of joy, laughter and happiness in the Lord, you are stronger in every way? You feel more energized. You are hopeful and motivated. The joy God gives us is our strength.

1. Nehemiah 8:10-12

    Underline the words "joy" and "mirth."

    > *Then he said unto them, Go your way, eat the fat, and drink the*
    > *sweet, and send portions unto them for whom nothing is prepared:*
    > *for this day is holy unto our LORD: neither be ye sorry; for the joy*
    > *of the LORD is your strength. So the Levites stilled all the people,*
    > *saying, Hold your peace, for the day is holy; neither be ye grieved.*
    > *And all the people went their way to eat, and to drink, and to send*
    > *portions, and to make great mirth, because they had understood*
    > *the words that were declared unto them. (KJV)*

    According to this passage, what is our strength?

    Why do you think the joy of the Lord gives us strength?

    Nehemiah told the people to rejoice in God's goodness. He told them to celebrate, change their thinking, eat feast foods and give gifts to others. A spirit of celebration accompanies the joy of the Lord.

    In verse 12, what did the people do?

    NUGGET: Notice that the people made a choice to celebrate with joy. The King James Version of the Bible says they decided to "make great mirth." I love that! When was the last time you just decided to make great mirth? There is a lot of truth to the old song, "Don't worry; be happy." Joy is attractive! Joy is fun! Joy is refreshing! Often we have to stir this up and make ourselves rejoice.

Describe ways that you can begin to "make mirth."

Whether it's small, natural things or big, spiritual things, we can make mirth. What refreshes you? What brightens your moment? How can you celebrate and stir up the joy of the Lord? Is it a thirty minute walk? Coffee with a friend? A new tube of lip gloss or a fishing magazine? Is it alone time with God? Organizing a cluttered drawer? Shopping? A massage? Singing? Prayer and God's Presence? A funny movie? Watching the sunset? What is it for you? Make mirth!

NUGGET: In this story in Nehemiah, when the people were wrongly interpreting the Word of the Lord, they were sad and depressed. When Nehemiah, Ezra and the Levites helped them to correctly interpret what the Word of the Lord meant, it brought great joy. Maybe you should take a moment to evaluate the things you are hearing. If you are reading books, listening to sermons or songs that are causing you to be overly introspective, depressed, sad and distressed, it's likely that those things are not in agreement with God's Word. Unfortunately, some preachers preach the Bible as if it were bad news. Certainly, there are some sober truths in God's Word, but for those walking with God in the light of His Word, there is fullness of joy. Jesus said God's Word and His plans are Good News, and in most cases, good news brings great joy!

I encourage you to take inventory of the things you are listening to or watching. Make sure you are listening to music and sitting under ministers who are preaching the Word so you will experience the life and joy God's Word brings. God's Word is a delight and a cause for rejoicing in our hearts, if we will let it be. If you believe God's Word and take Him at His Word, it is absolutely thrilling!

2. Psalm 45:7, Hebrews 1:9

   In these verses, underline the anointing God endowed Jesus with. Circle the things we are to love and hate.

   > *You love righteousness and hate wickedness; therefore God, Your God, has anointed You with the oil of gladness more than Your companions. (Psalm 45:7, NKJV)*

   > *You have loved righteousness and hated lawlessness; therefore God, Your God, has anointed You with the oil of gladness more than Your companions. (Hebrews 1:9, NKJV)*

   What was Jesus anointed with?

   NUGGET: Jesus was anointed with gladness. Many people view Jesus as a sober, somber, serious person. No, Jesus had more joy than anyone else, according to these passages. Isn't that awesome! He was not angry, sad, mad, introspective, depressed or discouraged. I can imagine Jesus walking around with radiant joy and a spirit of gladness as He talked with people and ministered to them. Gladness is a sign of spiritual maturity. The Bible says Jesus was anointed with the oil of gladness, more than anyone else. Jesus was and is a happy, full-of-joy, kind of person—and we can be just like Him!

   Why did God anoint Jesus with such gladness, according to this verse?

3. John 15:9-11, 16:23-24

   Underline the phrase "your joy may be full."

As the Father loved Me, I also have loved you; abide in My love. If you keep My commandments, you will abide in My love, just as I have kept My Father's commandments and abide in His love. These things I have spoken to you, that My joy may remain in you, and that your joy may be full. (NKJV)

And in that day you will ask Me nothing. Most assuredly, I say to you, whatever you ask the Father in My name He will give you. Until now you have asked nothing in My name. Ask, and you will receive, that your joy may be full. (NKJV)

Whose joy does Jesus want us to have?

How much joy does He want us to have?

What did Jesus say would give us His joy?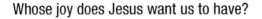

How would you define the phrase "your joy may be full"?

4. 1 Peter 1:8

Underline the adjectives that describe the joy of the believer.

You love him even though you have never seen him. Though you do not see him now, you trust him; and now you rejoice with a glorious, inexpressible joy. (NLT)

As someone who believes and knows and trusts Jesus personally, what is your heart filled with?

5. Philippians 4:4

   Underline the word that tells us when to be full of joy.

   Always be full of joy in the Lord. I say it again—rejoice! (NLT)

   According to this verse, when is it okay to be depressed?

   To be full of the joy of the Lord, what are we to do?

6. Psalm 16:11

   Underline the phrase "fullness of joy."

   You will show me the path of life; in Your presence is fullness of joy; at Your right hand are pleasures forevermore. (NKJV)

   Where do we find fullness of joy?

   What is at God's right hand?

NUGGET: God's Presence is a good place to hang out! You can tell when people spend time in God's Presence, because their life is marked by fullness of joy. After all, the Apostle Paul, inspired by the Holy Spirit told us, *"The kingdom of God is not eating and drinking, but righteousness and peace and joy in the Holy Spirit"* (Romans 14:17, NKJV). If you consider yourself to be a mature, spiritually developed person and your life is full of soberness, seriousness and a stoic disposition, you may want to spend more time meditating on God's Word and His promise of fullness of joy and gladness. Remember, Jesus was God's Son and He was anointed with the oil of gladness. When we spend time with God our Father, Jesus and the Holy Spirit, He will anoint us with joy and gladness, too!

Laugh a Lot

Laughter is good for you! It's just impossible to be sad, depressed, bummed, blue or in the dumps if you cultivate a life of laughter. When was the last time you had a real hearty, refreshing laugh?

1. Proverbs 15:13

    Underline the thing that gives us a pretty face.

    > *A happy heart makes the face cheerful, but heartache crushes the spirit. (NIV)*

    What does a happy heart do for your face?

Want to look younger? Laugh! Happiness and joy light up your face!

2. Proverbs 15:15

   Underline the secret to a life full of feasting.

   > *All the days of the oppressed are wretched, but the cheerful heart has a continual feast. (NIV)*

   What kind of days do those who are oppressed with depression have?

   What do the cheerful enjoy?

   Notice, this is your choice! Which would you prefer—wretched days or a continual feast?

3. Proverbs 17:22

   Underline the result of a cheerful heart.

   > *A cheerful heart is good medicine, but a crushed spirit dries up the bones. (NIV)*

   If you're thinking of being medicated for depression, have you considered this type of medication as well?

   The Message Bible makes it clear: *"A cheerful disposition is good for your health; gloom and doom leave you bone-tired" (The Message).*

What does a cheerful heart or a cheerful disposition do for you?

What does doom, gloom and having the blues do to you?

Everyone in medical science doesn't agree with God's Word on this subject. But there have been numerous people who have testified to the healing properties of laughter. Not all of these people have been Christians, but is it possible that they have tapped into something that the Lord told us in His Word thousands of years ago?

NUGGET: Researchers tell us what we already knew instinctively about laughter and health, *"We've long known that the ability to laugh is helpful to those coping with major illness and the stress of life's problems. But researchers are now saying laughter can do a lot more—it can basically bring balance to all the components of the immune system, which helps us fight off diseases . . . laughter reduces levels of certain stress hormones. In doing this, laughter provides a safety valve that shuts off the flow of stress hormones and the fight-or-flight compounds that swing into action in our bodies when we experience stress, anger or hostility. These stress hormones suppress the immune system, increase the number of blood platelets (which can cause obstructions in arteries) and raise blood pressure. When we're laughing, natural killer cells that destroy tumors and viruses increase, as do Gamma-interferon (a disease-fighting protein), T-cells (a major part of the immune response) and B-cells, which make disease-destroying antibodies . . . What may surprise you even more is the fact that researchers estimate that laughing 100 times is equal to 10 minutes on the rowing machine or 15 minutes on an exercise bike. Laughing can be a total body workout! Blood pressure is lowered, and there is an increase in vascular blood flow and in oxygenation of the blood, which further assists healing. Laughter also gives your diaphragm and abdominal, respiratory, facial, leg and back muscles a workout. That's why you often feel exhausted after a long bout of laughter—you've just had an aerobic workout!"*[1]

The psychological benefits of humor are amazing, according to doctors and nurses who are members of the American Association for Therapeutic Humor. People often store negative emotions, such as anger, sadness and fear, rather than expressing them. Laughter provides a way for these emotions to be harmlessly released. Laughter is cathartic. That's why some people who are upset or stressed out go to a funny movie or a comedy club. They laugh the negative emotions away. These negative emotions, when held inside, can cause biochemical changes that can affect our bodies.[2]

Here are some natural tips to help you put more laughter in your life:

- Figure out what makes you laugh and do it (or read it or watch it) more often. Funny movies, books and stories are a great source for priming the laughter pump.

- Surround yourself with funny people—be with them every chance you get.

- Develop your own sense of humor. Look for ways to make others laugh. Find the light side and the bright side of every situation.

- Just start laughing and praising God, as a matter of choice on purpose. You'll be surprised by how refreshing it will be.

Norman Cousins' 1979 book, *Anatomy of an Illness*, brought the idea of laughter and healing to the forefront.[3] He was suffering from ankylosing spondylitis, a degenerative spinal disease which put him in almost constant pain. He decided to watch comedy films and laugh a lot. He discovered that as little as ten minutes of laughter would give him two hours of pain-free sleep.

The explanation for why laughter reduces pain is not yet clear. While most people assume it's because of the production of endorphins (one of the body's natural pain killers), there is still no scientific evidence to support this view. The reduced pain may also be explained by the muscle relaxation that occurs from laughter, or because humor and laughter distract us from the source of pain.

God knew all of this long ago when He told us that *"a merry heart does good like a medicine."* Make the choice to be joyful, even in the midst of contrary circumstances and you'll be strengthened and lifted up!

4. Psalm 126:1-3

Underline the words "dreamed," "laughter," and "joy."

> *When the LORD brought back the captives to Zion, we were like men who dreamed. Our mouths were filled with laughter, our tongues with songs of joy. Then it was said among the nations, "The LORD has done great things for them." The LORD has done great things for us, and we are filled with joy. (NIV)*

Has God ever released you from captivity? Sin? Habits? Bondage?

What is the automatic and courteous response when someone sets you free?

If Jesus has freed you from any bondage, then it is time to fill your mouth with laughter and songs of joy! Start declaring how good God has been

UP

to you and you will find His goodness overflowing into more and more areas of your life.

5. Genesis 17:19

Underline the phrase "call his name Isaac [laughter]."

> But God said, Sarah your wife shall bear you a son indeed, and you shall call his name Isaac [laughter]; and I will establish My covenant or solemn pledge with him for an everlasting covenant and with his posterity after him. (AMP)

What did God choose to name Abraham and Sarah's son of promise?

Isn't that interesting? Through Isaac's name, God wanted us to be reminded down through the ages of His will for us to laugh and rejoice in the certainty of His promises. With a name like Laughter, you just cannot be sad or depressed on a regular basis. Isaac, Laughter, cannot be sad. It's just not congruent. What do you call yourself? Let's hope it's not Grumpy, Dopey or Downer. Perhaps you need to give yourself a joy-filled nickname and begin calling yourself Happy, Laughter, Joyful, Giggles, Bubbly, Smiley, Upbeat or Glad!

Sing a Song

Finally, let me mention the idea of singing songs of joy. Singing songs of joy from your heart will do more to lift your spirit than just about anything. Did you know that you can sing songs out of your heart? As the Lord gives you words, just sing them out!

1. Ephesians 5:18-20

Underline the words "sing/singing" and "song/songs."

Don't drink too much wine. That cheapens your life. Drink the Spirit of God, huge draughts of him. Sing hymns instead of drinking songs! Sing songs from your heart to Christ. Sing praises over everything, any excuse for a song to God the Father in the name of our Master, Jesus Christ. (The Message)

NUGGET: Have you ever noticed photographs of people who are drunk? They usually look very happy, hilarious and joyful, right? When people are intoxicated with alcohol, they often sing songs, laugh and act happy—the only problem is that it's a counterfeit happiness and doesn't last. God has something better. He wants us to live under the influence—of Him! He wants us to be intoxicated with His goodness. God wants us to enjoy the freedom, laughter and joy that come from being "drunk" in Him. Get intoxicated with God and His Word! Living under His influence will fill your heart and mouth with songs of joy and gladness.

What are we supposed to drink?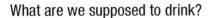

What are we supposed to sing?

Where do songs originate within us?

NUGGET: Hymns and spiritual songs don't have to sound like a dirge! God knows the style of music that will minister to your heart—it's not the beat or sound that is so important, it's the words. It doesn't matter if you sing songs that sound like country, R&B, rock and roll, rap or top 40. Just sing words that are congruent with His Word from your heart. Put together a playlist of songs that lift up your spirit with joy and songs that cause your soul to be happy, and sing them regularly. Make up your own songs by singing of your thanks to God. Make up the words as you go and you'll find that the Lord will fill your heart and mouth with phrases and melodies!

2. Psalm 126:5-6

Underline the phrase "songs of joy."

> *Those who sow in tears will reap with songs of joy. He who goes out weeping, carrying seed to sow, will return with songs of joy, carrying sheaves with him. (NIV)*

Perhaps as you and I pray and sow seeds of prayer, faith, giving and witnessing, there is a season of tears and earnestness. But what does God promise in the end?

When we reap, what type of songs are we to sing?

3. Psalm 32:7

> *You are my hiding place; you will protect me from trouble and surround me with songs of deliverance. (NIV)*

How would you describe a "song of deliverance"?

Why not make a decision to sing a song of deliverance from depression and discouragement? Let the Lord give you words from your heart, then begin to sing them out by faith. You'll be blessed by the reality of deliverance!

Scriptures to Meditate On

Though you have not seen him, you love him;
and even though you do not see him now, you believe in him
and are filled with an inexpressible and glorious joy.

1 Peter 1:8, NIV

The joy of the LORD is your strength.

Nehemiah 8:10, NKJV

Group Discussion

1. Describe your "happy place." What do you do in your own personal life and walk with God to make mirth and find the place of joy, laughter and singing?

2. Give each person in your small group a nickname that describes joy, happiness and laughter. Be creative!

3. Find a photo of yourself laughing and post this snapshot in a place where you can view it on a regular basis. Share this photo with your small group and describe the circumstances of the photo.

---

[1] Marshall, Brian, "How Laughter Works, "*Howstuffworks.com*", science.howstuffworks. com/life/laughter6.htm.

[2] *http://www.aath.org*

[3] Norman, Cousins, *Anatomy of an Illness,*(New York: W.W. Norton & Co., 1995)

CHAPTER 5
You've Got To Have Friends

Sing it!

Do you remember any of these oldies? *"You've got to have frieeeends!"* Bette Midler and Barry Manilow both told us so! Carole King promised we could lean on her, *". . . when you're not strong and I'll be your friend, I'll help you carry on . . ."* *"Just look over your shoulder honey, I'll be there . . ."*, thank you Jackson Five! Carly Simon and James Taylor told us, *"Winter, spring, summer or fall all you have to do is call and I'll be there, yes I will, you've got a friend . . ."* Michael W. Smith reminded us, *"Friends are friends forever when the Lord's the Lord of them . . ."* Barbara Streisand summed it up, *"People who need people are the luckiest people . . ."* Are you one of those blessed people? Is friendship something you cultivate?

Three Dog Night had it right: *One is the loneliest number!* We need friends and good friends are a gift from God. Jesus is our best friend; He sticks closer than a brother. He's our first love, but because He knows the value of godly relationships, He brings us together with people in His family in such a way that He provides divine, God-breathed, God-ordained, God-knit friendships.

It's amazing what lunch with a friend, a heartfelt e-mail, a funny card, a word of encouragement from a friend or even a simple "like" on social media will do to lift your spirit up. Let's look at the power of friendship.

God-Knit Friends

1. 2 Corinthians 7:6

> Underline the words "comfort/ed," "encourages/ed," "refreshes/ed" and "cheers/ed."

> *But God, Who comforts and encourages and refreshes and cheers the depressed and the sinking, comforted and encouraged and refreshed and cheered us by the arrival of Titus. (AMP)*

What does God do for us?

What did the arrival of Titus, Paul's friend, do for Paul?

It's amazing how the right person at the right time can be used of God to comfort, encourage, refresh and cheer us up from the place of depression.

Who has encouraged you lately?

Who have you encouraged lately?

2. Romans 15:30-32

   Underline the thing that results when we have God-ordained relationships.

   > *Will you be my prayer partners? For the Lord Jesus Christ's sake and because of your love for me-given to you by the Holy Spirit-pray much with me for my work. Pray that I will be protected in Jerusalem from those who are not Christians. Pray also that the Christians there will be willing to accept the money I am bringing them. Then I will be able to come to you with a happy heart by the will of God, and we can refresh each other. (TLB)*

   What did Paul need from his friends?

   In verse 32, what did Paul say would happen for him and his friends when, by God's will, they were united?

3. 1 Corinthians 16:17-18, 2 Corinthians 7:13

   Underline the word "refreshed."

   > *I was glad when Stephanas, Fortunatus and Achaicus arrived, because they have supplied what was lacking from you. For they refreshed my spirit and yours also. Such men deserve recognition. (1 Corinthians 16:17-18, NIV)*

   > *By all this we are encouraged. In addition to our own encouragement, we were especially delighted to see how happy Titus was, because his spirit has been refreshed by all of you. (2 Corinthians 7:13-14, NIV)*

What does getting together with godly friends do for your spirit?

4. 2 Timothy 1:16-18

   Underline the phrases that describe the way Onesiphorus encouraged Paul.

   > *The Lord grant mercy to the household of Onesiphorus, for he often refreshed me, and was not ashamed of my chain; but when he arrived in Rome, he sought me out very zealously and found me. The Lord grant to him that he may find mercy from the Lord in that Day—and you know very well how many ways he ministered to me at Ephesus. (NKJV)*

   Paul was facing persecution and discouragement. Describe the way Onesiphorus encouraged Paul.

5. Philemon 1:7

   Underline the words that describe the encouragement Paul received from his Christian friends.

   > *For I have derived great joy and comfort and encouragement from your love, because the hearts of the saints [who are your fellow Christians] have been cheered and refreshed through you, [my] brother. (AMP)*

   A godly friend is a gift. What does a friend do?

6. Exodus 17:12

    Underline the key word that describes Aaron and Hur's help for Moses.

    > *But Moses' hands became heavy; so they took a stone and put it under him, and he sat on it. And Aaron and Hur supported his hands, one on one side, and the other on the other side; and his hands were steady until the going down of the sun. (NKJV)*

    What role did Aaron and Hur play in helping Moses?

    Do you have a support system in your life?

    List those friends who are in your support system:

7. Proverbs 12:25

    Underline one of the causes of depression and one of the cures.

    > *Anxiety in the heart of man causes depression, but a good word makes it glad. (NKJV)*

    What does a good word do for us?

Who gave you your last good word?

8. Ephesians 4:29

   In this verse, underline the type of words that are not encouraging.

   > *Let no foul or polluting language, nor evil word nor unwhole-*
   > *some or worthless talk [ever] come out of your mouth, but*
   > *only such [speech] as is good and beneficial to the spiritual*
   > *progress of others, as is fitting to the need and the occasion,*
   > *that it may be a blessing and give grace (God's favor) to those*
   > *who hear it. (AMP)*

   What kinds of words do we need to speak to others?

   What do such words impart?

   A supernatural deposit of grace is given to us when we choose to speak wholesome words that edify and build others up; grace to overcome depression.

   Do you have friends who lift you up? Do you lift up your friends? If you need to improve in these areas, why not ask God right now for friends who will lift you up and ask Him to help you to be a better friend in lifting up others.

Scriptures to Meditate On

A man who has friends must himself be friendly,
But there is a friend who sticks closer than a brother.

Proverbs 18:24, NKJV

Reliable friends who do what they say
are like cool drinks in sweltering heat—refreshing!

Proverbs 25:13, The Message

Group Discussion

1. Describe some of the significant times in your life when friends encouraged and lifted you up.

2. Describe the importance of and challenges in having a support system. Talk about your current support system—what three people would you call on in a time of need? Are you a part of anyone's support system?

   In other words, who would call you?

3. Describe the importance of being in a small group or having a small circle of friends, and the ways you have found encouragement through one another.

CHAPTER 6
Lift Up the Down

We were never created to do life alone. We need the family of God to encourage us, counsel us, pray for us, exhort us, correct us and help us—and we need to do those things for others. You've heard it many times: *"Do unto others as you would have them do unto you."* Jesus said it, and your mother drilled it into your ears. It's true. One of the best ways to find your own spirit lifted up is to lift up those around you. When we focus on meeting the needs of others, it tends to distract us from our own issues and helps put things into perspective.

Encourage Others

1. 2 Corinthians 1:3-5

    In this passage, underline the words "compassion" and "comfort."

    > *Praise be to the God and Father of our Lord Jesus Christ, the Father of compassion and the God of all comfort, who comforts us in all our troubles, so that we can comfort those in any trouble with the comfort we ourselves have received from God. For just as the sufferings of Christ flow over into our lives, so also through Christ our comfort overflows. (NIV)*

    All compassion and comfort comes from whom?

Has God ever comforted you in a time of trouble, disappointment or depression?

We are carriers of God's comfort.

What are we to do for others?

What are some ways you can comfort and encourage someone who is down in the dumps?

2. Acts 4:36

Underline Barnabas' nickname.

> *Joseph, a Levite from Cyprus, whom the apostles called Barnabas (which means Son of Encouragement). (NIV)*

What was Barnabas' nickname?

Why do you think he earned this name?

If someone had to give you a nickname, what would people call you?

3. Romans 15:5-6

   In this passage, underline the words that describe encouragement and harmony in relationships.

   > *Now may the God of patience and comfort grant you to be like-minded toward one another, according to Christ Jesus, that you may with one mind and one mouth glorify the God and Father of our Lord Jesus Christ. (NKJV)*

   What can we ask God to give us?

   For what purpose?

   Let's have the same heart to encourage one another that God has t o - ward encouraging us!

4. Philippians 2:1-5

   In this passage, underline the way we should treat one another.

   > *If you have any encouragement from being united with Christ, if any comfort from his love, if any fellowship with the Spirit, if any tenderness and compassion, then make my joy complete by being like-minded, having the same love, being one in spirit and purpose. Do nothing out of selfish ambition or vain conceit, but in humility consider others better than your-*

*selves. Each of you should look not only to your own inter-
ests, but also to the interests of others. Your attitude should
be the same as that of Christ Jesus. (NIV)*

If we are united with Christ, we have plenty to be encouraged about!

How can we make the Lord's joy complete?

What does verse 4 tell us to do?

5. Ephesians 4:29

Underline the phrase "building others up."

*Do not let any unwholesome talk come out of your mouths,
but only what is helpful for building others up according to
their needs, that it may benefit those who listen. (NIV)*

What is one primary way we build others up?

Once again, think about the words you say to others. It's an amazing
thing to think of our words as carriers. They can carry life or death, blessing or cursing, encouragement or discouragement. We can build up or
tear down. Put your mouth to work in lifting others up!

Friends Love Each Other

1. 1 John 3:11

    Underline what we are to do for one another.

    > *For this is the message that you heard from the beginning, that we should love one another. (NKJV)*

    What is God's message from the beginning?

2. John 13:34-35

    Underline the new commandment.

    > *A new commandment I give to you, that you love one another; as I have loved you, that you also love one another. By this all will know that you are My disciples, if you have love for one another. (NKJV)*

    How are we to love one another?

    What will people see when we love one another?

3. 1 John 4:7-8

Underline the word "love."

> *Dear friends, let us love one another, for love comes from God. Everyone who loves has been born of God and knows God. Whoever does not love does not know God, because God is love. (NIV)*

What are we supposed to do for one another?

Who is the author of love?

If we are born of God—born again—what do we do?

4. Romans 12:9-15

Underline the phrase "Love from the center of who you are."

> *Love from the center of who you are; don't fake it. Run for dear life from evil; hold on for dear life to good. Be good friends who love deeply; practice playing second fiddle. Don't burn out; keep yourselves fueled and aflame. Be alert servants of the Master, cheerfully expectant. Don't quit in hard times; pray all the harder. Help needy Christians; be inventive in hospitality. Bless your enemies; no cursing under your breath. Laugh with your happy friends when they're happy; share tears when they're down. (The Message)*

What does the Lord tell us not to fake?

What do good friends do?

What are we to do when our friends are down?

5. 1 Corinthians 13:4-8

Underline the word "love."

> *Love endures long and is patient and kind; love never is envious nor boils over with jealousy, is not boastful or vainglorious, does not display itself haughtily. It is not conceited (arrogant and inflated with pride); it is not rude (unmannerly) and does not act unbecomingly. Love (God's love in us) does not insist on its own rights or its own way, for it is not self-seeking; it is not touchy or fretful or resentful; it takes no account of the evil done to it [it pays no attention to a suffered wrong]. It does not rejoice at injustice and unrighteousness, but rejoices when right and truth prevail. Love bears up under anything and everything that comes, is ever ready to believe the best of every person, its hopes are fadeless under all circumstances, and it endures everything [without weakening]. Love never fails [never fades out or becomes obsolete or comes to an end]. (AMP)*

This passage of Scripture always hits home. Loving others is a noble thought, but 1 Corinthians 13 really makes it practical.

In what ways do you find you struggle with this passage?

What area are you going to focus on improving?

What does verse 8 promise you?

List the 25-27 different components to walking in love according to this Amplified version of 1 Corinthians 13.

I encourage you to memorize this passage and make it your life mission. Jesus said the greatest commandment is to love God and to love our neighbor as ourselves, and 1 Corinthians 13 tells us how to do it.

Make it your goal to be on the lookout for someone who needs encouragement and comfort. You can be used of God to help lift them out of the blues. Cry with those who are crying. Love them deeply. Speak words that will build them up. Have fun hunting for someone to bless!

Scriptures to Meditate On

Those who say they live in God should live their lives as Jesus did.

1 John 2:6, NLT

And as we live in God, our love grows more perfect.
So we will not be afraid on the day of judgment,
but we can face him with confidence
because we live like Jesus here in this world.

1 John 4:17, NLT

Group Discussion

1. Describe a time in your life when your encouragement lifted up another. What did you do to encourage this person?

2. Describe the challenge of encouraging and lifting up those who are discouraged and depressed. How do you handle it when they do not respond immediately? What have you learned about being patient and consistent?

3. Describe the power of 1 Corinthians 13. Which phrase in this passage challenges you the most?

Notes

Notes

Notes

Notes

Notes

ABOUT THE AUTHOR
Beth Jones

Beth Jones and her husband Jeff are the founders and senior pastors of Valley Family Church in Kalamazoo, Michigan, planted in 1991 and named by Outreach magazine as one of the fastest growing churches in America in 2009 and 2010. They also lead Jeff and Beth Jones Ministries, an organization dedicated to helping people *get the basics.* Beth and Jeff have four children who are all involved in leadership and ministry.

Beth grew up in Lansing, Michigan, and was raised as a Catholic. At the end of her freshman year in college, she came into a personal relationship with Christ through the testimony of her roommate. It was there, at age 19, that she realized God's plan for her to preach and teach the gospel through writing and speaking. She has been following that call ever since.

Beth is the author of 20 books, including the popular *Getting a Grip on the Basics* series, which is being used by thousands of churches in America and has been translated into over a dozen foreign languages and used around the world. She also writes *The Basics Daily Devo,* a free daily edevotional for thousands of subscribers.

The heart of Beth's message is simple: *"I exist to help people get the basics!"* Through her practical, down-to-earth teaching, she inspires people to enjoy an authentic relationship with Jesus, to take Him at His Word, and to reach their greatest God-given potential!

Beth attended Boston University in Boston, Massachusetts and received her ministry training at Rhema Bible Training Center in Tulsa, Oklahoma.

For more spiritual growth resources or to connect with Beth, please visit:

www.valleyfamilychurch.org

www.jeffandbethjones.com

www.facebook.com/jeffandbethjones

www.twitter.com/bethjones

www.instagram.com/bethjones

PRAYER OF SALVATION

God loves you—no matter who you are, no matter what your past. God loves you so much that He gave His one and only begotten Son for you. The Bible tells us that "...whoever believes in Him shall not perish but have eternal life" (John 3:16 NIV). Jesus laid down His life and rose again so that we could spend eternity with Him in heaven and experience His absolute best on earth. If you would like to receive Jesus into your life, say the following prayer out loud and mean it from your heart.

Heavenly Father, I come to You admitting that I am a sinner. Right now, I choose to turn away from sin, and I ask You to cleanse me of all unrighteousness. I believe that Your Son, Jesus, died on the cross to take away my sins. I also believe that He rose again from the dead so that I might be forgiven of my sins and made righteous through faith in Him. I call upon the name of Jesus Christ to be the Savior and Lord of my life. Jesus, I choose to follow You and ask that You fill me with the power of the Holy Spirit. I declare that right now I am a child of God. I am free from sin and full of the right-eousness of God. I am saved in Jesus' name. Amen.

If you prayed this prayer to receive Jesus Christ as your Savior for the first time, please contact us on the Web at **www.harrisonhouse.com** to receive a free book.

Or you may write to us at
Harrison House • P.O. Box 35035 • Tulsa, Oklahoma 74153

The Harrison House Vision

Proclaiming the truth and the power

Of the Gospel of Jesus Christ

With excellence;

Challenging Christians to

Live victoriously,

Grow spiritually,

Know God intimately.